The

Pursuit

of

Wisdom

The Pursuit of Wisdom

One definition of wisdom is the ability to deal successfully with the affairs of life.

With this definition in mind does it not make sense for any person no matter what station in life they are in, to make the seeking of wisdom a top priority?

This has been called the information age, yet for all the information that is available to us, people are still making the same mistakes that people have been making for thousands of years. Why is that? I believe it is because they lack wisdom.

Wisdom anticipates future circumstances we will face.

Wisdom prepares us for the decisions we will make in the future. It gives us a basis for making better decisions and that can make the difference between making good and bad choices. We cannot eliminate making bad decisions but we can minimize them.

Wisdom comes from experience, observation and deep thought. Wisdom must be sought after.

It can be found among all people and cultures, rich and poor alike, in every part of the world, and throughout the history of mankind.

No person, group of people, culture, nation or time period has a monopoly on wisdom, rather it may be found spread out throughout the world and from ancient times.

Is wisdom attainable by the average person?
Absolutely.

Wise men of old found that the best way to communicate wisdom to others is through the use of short sayings or proverbs. You will be amazed at how much you will learn if you will just spend a few minutes every day reading and thinking about what is said in these proverbs and sayings that have come down to us through the ages. They have a way of making their way back to your mind at the appropriate time.

Some of these quotes, sayings and proverbs will amuse you, some will make you think, some will state the obvious, but one thing is for sure they will change your thinking and your outlook upon life.

On The Pursuit Of Wisdom

King Solomon is widely known for his wisdom. One of the things he said about wisdom is that it is a life-long pursuit, as a matter of fact he made the pursuit of wisdom his life work, gathering and teaching wisdom.

And he spake three thousand proverbs: and his songs were a thousand and five.
                                        1 Kings 4:32

The Teacher was very wise and taught the people what he knew. He very carefully thought about, studied, and set in order many wise teachings. The Teacher looked for just the right words to write what is dependable and true.
                                        Eccl. 12:9-10

One of the greatest things we learn from his example and teachings is that if we seek wisdom instead of other things, wisdom will give us the other things we desire.

The man who knows right from wrong and has good judgment and common sense is happier than the man who is immensely rich!
For such wisdom is far more valuable than precious jewels. Nothing else compares with it.
Wisdom gives: a long, good life, riches, honor, pleasure, peace.
Wisdom is a tree of life to those who eat her fruit; happy is the man who keeps on eating it.
Prov. 3:13-18 TLB

King Solomon knew what he was talking about, he had no equal in his lifetime, he was tremendously wealthy and his kingdom had no rival. What was his secret to all his success? He reveals it in his writings, it was his pursuit of wisdom.

7 Wisdom is the principal thing; therefore get wisdom: and with all thy getting get understanding.
8 Exalt her, and she shall promote thee: she shall bring thee to honour, when thou dost embrace her.
9 She shall give to thine head an ornament of grace: a crown of glory shall she deliver to thee.
Prov. 4:7-9

And the king made silver and gold at Jerusalem as plenteous as stones, and cedar trees made he as the sycomore trees that are in the vale for abundance.
2 Chr. 1:15

Many years ago I became fascinated with the story of King Solomon and what he had to say about the benefits of seeking wisdom. I decided that I too would become a seeker of wisdom. I soon became discouraged because I, like so many other people mistake wisdom with just acquiring knowledge from much study.

Until one day a few years ago it dawned upon me the method wisdom was communicated from the wise men of old to their students, it was through proverbs, sayings, quotes and short lines of wit. Now that I knew how to get wisdom it was only a matter of finding it, so my pursuit began.

Different people collect proverbs, quotes, sayings for different reasons, some appreciate what they say, others such as writers and speakers use them in their work. I believe anyone can benefit from reading and meditating upon them, you will acquire wisdom in this way.

This book contains a portion of the proverbs, sayings, wit and wisdom I have gathered over these past few years. It represents my pursuit for wisdom. I would like to encourage you the reader to begin your own pursuit for wisdom, make it a daily task, you will be glad you did. This book will help you get started.

"...The quotation when engraved upon the memory give you good thoughts."

-Winston Churchill

The fear of the Lord is the beginning of wisdom: and the knowledge of the holy is understanding.

-King Solomon

Living without an aim is like sailing without a compass.

-Alexander Dumas

A journey of a thousand miles must begin with a single step.   -Lao Tzu

The art of being wise is the art of knowing what to overlook.   -William James

No one knows what he can do till he tries.   -Proverb

Whatever the mind of man can conceive and believe, it can achieve.   -Napoleon Hill

No man ever became wise by chance.   -Seneca

Nothing is said which has not been said before.   -Terrence

Indecisiveness breeds confusion.   -Chinese Proverb

Success isn't measured by the position you reach in life; it's measured by the obstacles you overcome.

-Booker T. Washington

Build your dreams or someone else will hire you to build theirs.   -Farrah Gray

Understanding is the reward of faith.   -St. Augustine

Discipline is the refining fire by which talent becomes ability.   -Roy L. Smith

Counsel after actions is like rain after harvest.

-Danish Proverb

Having children makes one no more a parent than having a piano makes you a pianist.   -Unknown

Anger is never without a reason, but seldom with a good one.   -Benjamin Franklin

The only thing some people do is grow old.

-Ed Howe

A rich child often sits in a poor mother's lap.

-Proverb

Our best successes often come after our greatest
disappointments. -Henry Ward Beecher

Say not always what you know, but always know what
you say. -Claudius

No gift to your mother can ever equal her gift to you.

-Unknown

Don't hit at all if you can help it; don't hit a man if you
can possibly avoid it; but if you do hit him, put him to
sleep. -Theodore Roosevelt

When a husband earns well, the wife spends well.

-Dutch Proverb

Fools live to regret their words, wise men to regret their silence.   -Will Henry

A jug fills drop by drop.   -Buddha

The most worthy calling in life is that in which man can serve best his fellow man.   -Unknown

Reckon loss before reckoning gain.   -Proverb

An uneasy conscience is a hair in the mouth.
    -Mark Twain

A grandparent is a living history lesson.
    -Old Saying

Everyone has talent; what is rare is the courage to follow the talent to the dark place where it leads.
    -Erica Jong

It is not wide reading but useful reading that tends to
excellence.   -Proverb

A sense of curiosity is nature's original school of
education.   -Smiley Blanton

Admit your errors before someone else exaggerates them.
          -Andrew V. Mason

In the long run, the pessimist may be proved right; but the
optimist has a better time on the trip.
          -Daniel L. Reardon

Just as our eyes need light in order to see, our minds
need ideas in order to conceive.   -Nicholas Malebranche

Live with him who prays and you will pray, live with him
who sings and you will sing.   -Arab Proverb

The most important thing that parents can teach their
children is how to get along without them.   -Unknown

In the end, it is important to remember that we cannot become what we need to be by remaining what we are.

-Max Dupree

Plenty of people are willing to give God credit, but few are willing to give Him cash.   -Anonymous

The heart like the stomach, wants a varied diet.

-Gustave Flaubert

The beaten road is the safest.   -Proverb

Home is a place you grow up wanting to leave, and grow old wanting to get back to.   -John Ed Pearce

A goal without a plan is just a wish.   -Unknown

Who gives to me teaches me to give.   -Dutch Proverb

The world stands aside to let anyone pass who knows where he is going.   -David Staff Jordan

If at first you don't succeed, failure may be your thing.

-Larry Anderson

All the darkness of the world cannot put out the light of one small candle. -Anon.

It is loving and giving that make life worth living.

-Unknown

There are forty kinds of lunacy, but only one kind of common sense. -African Proverb

No man can serve two masters, for either he will hate the one and love the other, or he will hold to one and despise the other. -Jesus

The one thing that doesn't abide by majority rule is a person's conscience. -Harper Lee

Choice is the strongest principle of growth.

-George Eliot

It is impossible to defeat an ignorant man in argument.

-William G. McAdoo

A hospital should also have a recovery room adjoining the cashier's office.   -Francis O'Walsh

Many receive advice, only the wise profit by it.

-Proverb

The guest is dearest when he is leaving.

-German Proverb

My works are like water. The works of the great masters are like wine. But everyone drinks water.

-Mark Twain

Some people are always grumbling because roses have thorns; I am thankful that thorns have roses.

-Alphonse Karr

Pride and prejudice are brothers.   -Chinese Proverb

Practice without improvement is meaningless.

-Chuck Knox

Example is not the main thing in influencing others. It is the only thing.   -Albert Schweitzer

Those who deserve love the least need it the most.

-Old Saying

Millions long for immortality who do not know what to do with themselves on a rainy Sunday afternoon.

-Susan Ertz

After crosses and losses men grow humbler and wiser.

-Benjamin Franklin

One gets pearls without asking, and another cannot obtain alms even by begging.   -Proverb

There is a foolish corner in the brain of the wisest man.

-Aristole

Don't stand shivering upon the bank; plunge in at once, and have it over.　　　-Sam Slick

A lover's faults do not bother you.　　　-Old Saying

There is no act, however trivial, but has its train of consequences.　　　-Samuel Smiles

The sleep of a laboring man is sweet.

　　-King Solomon

Books are still man's greatest invention, despite the nonsense so often published between their covers.

　　-Martin Arnold

To accomplish great things, we must not only act, but also dream; not only plan, but also believe.

　　-Anatole France

A pair of good ears will drain dry a hundred tongues.
　　-Proverb

He who would climb the ladder must begin at the bottom.

-Proverb

He has only half learned the art of reading who has not added to it the more refined art of skipping and skimming.

-Arthur James Balfour

To a fool the ocean is only knee deep.

-Russian Proverb

It is amazing how complete is the delusion that beauty is goodness.   -Leo Tolstoy

Happiness lies not in the mere possession of money, it lies in the joy of achievement in the thrill of creative effort.

-Franklin D. Roosevelt

Feeling gratitude and not expressing it is like wrapping a present and not giving it.   -William Arthur Ward

Give according to your income, lest God make your income according to your giving.   -Peter Marshall

Mothers are like fine collectibles – as the years go by, they increase in value.   -Unknown

Hell is paved with good intentions.   -Proverb

The best guide to conversation is to ask questions.

A good knowledge of history is a quiver full of arrows in debate.   -Winston Churchill

Prayer is the key of the morning and the lock of the evening.   -Gandhi

To extend your life by a year, take one fewer bite each meal.   -Chinese Proverb

One of the marks of true greatness is the ability to develop greatness in others   -J.C. Maccaulay

Wealth obtained by fraud dwindles, but the one who gathers by labor increases it.   -King Solomon

What we call failure is not the falling down, but the staying down.   -Mary Pickford

Patience wears out stones.   -Proverb

The older I grow the more I distrust the familiar doctrine that age brings wisdom.   -H.L. Mencken

Any plan that cannot be changed is a bad one.

   -Unknown

Many people will walk in and out of your life, but only true friends will leave footprints on your heart.

   -Eleanor Roosevelt

Insults are like bad coins; we cannot help being offered them, but we need not take them.   -Proverb

Go confidently in the direction of your dreams. Live the life you've imagined.   -Henry Thoreau

Forget injuries, never forget kindness.   -Confucius

Train your child in the way in which you know you should have gone yourself.   -Proverb

Cooking done with care is an act of love.

    -Craig Claiborne

Too much and too little education hinders the mind.

    -Proverb

The greatest of all faults, I should say, is to be conscious of none.   -Thomas Carlyle

Our envy always lasts longer than the happiness of those we envy.   -Heraclitus

A thing too much seen is little prized.   -French Proverb

Be not angry that you cannot make others as you wish them to be, since you cannot make yourself as you wish to be.   -Thomas Kempis

The important thing is not what they think of me, but what I think of them.   -Queen Victoria

Permit a man to light his fire from yours.   -Proverb

He also that is slothful in his work is brother to him that is a great waster.   -King Solomon

No one can make you feel inferior without your consent. Never give it.   -Eleanor Roosevelt

People are unreasonable, illogical, and self-centered. Love them anyway.   -Mother Teresa

There is no education like adversity.   -Proverb

The world is all gates, all opportunities strings of tension waiting to be struck.   -Ralph Waldo Emerson

Keeping company with the wicked is like living in a fish market; one becomes used to the foul odor.
     -Chinese Proverb

Daydreaming is wish craft.   -Bert Murray

A handful of common sense is worth a bushel of learning.
     -Spanish Proverb

Saying a thing is a thing, doesn't make a thing a thing.
     -Ross Williams

Every human being is intended to have a character of his own; to be what no others are, and to do what no other can do.   -Unknown

If we cannot learn wisdom from experience; it is hard to say where it is to be found.   -Thomas Jefferson

The devil divides the world between atheism and superstition.   -Herbert

The friend is the man who knows all about you, and still likes you.   -Elbert Hubbard

If we have not peace within ourselves, it is vain to seek it from outward sources.　　　　　-Rouchefoucauld

You cannot change truth, but truth can change you.
　　　-Proverb

It is in their leisure time that men are made or marred.
　　　-Will Taylor

Worry gives a small thing a big shadow.　　　-Proverb

Don't find fault. Find a remedy.　　　-Henry Ford

The shortest way to do many things is to do only one thing at a time.　　　-Cecil

They are ill discoveries that think there is no land, when they can see nothing but sea.　　　-Francis Bacon

Letters should be easy and natural.
　　　-Earl of Chesterfield

The secret of success is to do the common things uncommonly well.   -Unknown

Nature makes only dumb animals. We owe the fools to society.   -Honore de Balzac

To keep your secret is wisdom; but to expect others to keep it is folly.   -O.W. Holmes

When two elephants fight it is the grass that suffers.
          -African Proverb

Where parents do too much for their children, the children will not do much for themselves.   -Proverb

A good name is rather to be chosen than great riches.
          -King Solomon

I do myself a greater injury than I do him of whom I tell a lie.   -Michel de Montaigne

Choice is life's business.   -Robert Browning

Come not to counsel uncalled.   -Proverb

The best vision is insight.   -Malcolm S. Forbes

He who tells his wife all, is newly married.
-Scottish Proverb

Man tends to live on the level of the music he listens to.
Dr. Bob Smith

The roots grow deep when the winds are strong.
-Old Saying

Marriage is more than a wedding.   -Proverb

Joy shared is twice the joy. Sorrow shared is half the
sorrow.   -Proverbs

Let the first impulse pass, wait for the second.

-Baltasar Gracian

I am always doing that which I cannot do in order that I may learn how to do it. -Pablo Picasso

You may give without loving but you cannot love without giving. -Amy Carmichael

Twenty years from now you will be more disappointed by the things that you didn't do than by the ones you did do.
-Mark Twain

What the caterpillar calls the end of the world, the master calls a butterfly. -Proverb

You can have everything in life you want, if you will just help enough other people get what they want.
-Zig Ziglar

Good bargains empty your pockets. -German Proverb

Sin trills and sin kills. Sin fascinates, and then sin
assassinates.   -Sentence Sermon

If you would go far study the lives of men who have
achieved great things.   -Unknown

Common sense is the knack of seeing things as they are,
and doing things as they ought to be done.

           -Harriet Beecher Stowe

When wealth is lost nothing is lost; when health is lost
something is lost; when character is lost all is lost.

           -Billy Graham

If a little money does not go out, great money will not
come in.   -Chinese Proverb

Cheerfulness and contentment are great beautifiers and
are famous preservers of youthful looks.

           -Charles Dickens

Idleness and pride tax with a heavier hand than kings and
parliaments.   -Benjamin Franklin

It is what you learn after you think you know it all that counts.   -Harry S. Truman

It is always necessary to start from truth in order to teach an error.   -Mabel Newcomber

All doors open to courtesy.   -Thomas Fuller

It is part of the cure to wish to be cured.

    -Seneca

No choice is also a choice.   -Jewish Proverb

His heart cannot be pure whose tongue is not clean.

    -Anon.

There is no substitute for paying attention.   -Anon.

To ease another's heartache is to forget one's own.

    -Abraham Lincoln

Man, forget not death, for death certainly forgets not thee.

   -Anon.

Use the talents you possess; the woods would be very silent if no bird sang there except those that sang best.

   -Henry Van Dyke

Success is not a goal, but a means to aim still higher.

   -Unknown

Your ability to manage your time for maximum results is the core skill of personal effectiveness.
   -Brian Tracy

Learn to paddle your own boat.   -Old Saying

No gift to your mother can ever equal her gift to you.

   -Unknown

A soft answer turneth away wrath; but grievous words stir up anger.   -King Solomon

You will never make a more important decision than the person you marry.   -Unknown

The way to the top is to get off your bottom.

-Proverb

I'm a great believer in luck, and I find the harder I work, the more I have of it.   -Thomas Jefferson

He who does nothing makes no mistakes.

-Italian Proverb

Laughter is the tranquilizer with no side effects.

-Arnold Glasgow

Every man has a right to his opinion, but no man has a right to be wrong in his facts.   -Bernard Baruch

I have never been hurt by anything I didn't say.

-Unknown

Decency is like gold, the same in all countries.

-Li Hung-chang

Character is like a tree, and reputation is like its shadow. The shadow is what we think of it; the tree is the real thing.   -Unknown

The more you change the more you become an instrument of change in the lives of others.

-Howard Hendricks

Amusement is the happiness of those who cannot think.

-Alexander Pope

Appreciation is like an insurance policy. It has to be renewed every now and then.   -Dave McIntyre

No horse gets anywhere until he is harnessed. No life ever grows great until it is focused, dedicated, and disciplined.   -Unknown

Do not set fire to the forest to drive out the wolves.

-Chinese Proverb

The devil is sincere, but he is sincerely wrong.

-Billy Graham

It is more important to know where you are going than to see how fast you can get there.   -Unknown

Worry is like a rocking chair – it gives you something to do but gets you nowhere.   -Old Saying

Wealth consists not in having great possessions, but in having few wants.   -Epictetus

Definition of status: Buying something you don't need with money you don't have to impress people you don't like.   -Unknown

Eggs and oaths are easily broken.   -Danish Proverb

Go often to the house of a friend, for weeds choke the unused path. 						-Ralph Waldo Emerson

The anvil lasts longer than the hammer.

							-Italian Proverb

Economy is half the battle of life, it is not so hard to earn money as to spend it well. 						-Charles Spurgeon

To wait for someone else, or to expect someone else to make my life richer, or fuller, or more satisfying puts me in a constant state of suspension. 						-Kathleen Andrus

Grandparents are folks who come to your house, spoil your children then go home. 						-Unknown

A man who dares to waste one hour of life has not discovered the value of life. 						-Charles Darwin

When the ship has sunk, everyone knows how she could have been saved. 						-Italian Proverb

I have not failed. I've just found 10,000 ways that won't work.　　　-Thomas A. Edison

The apple falls not far from the tree.　　　-Proverb

Nobody can go back and start a new beginning, but anyone can start today and make a new ending.

　　　-Unknown

A person who never made a mistake never tried anything new.　　　-Albert Einstein

War is horrible, but slavery is worse.

　　　-Winston Churchill

Whoever loves money will never be contented with money. Whoever loves wealth will never be contented with more wealth.　　　-King Solomon

A truly rich man is one whose children run into his arms when his hands are empty.　　　-Unknown

A good laugh and a long sleep are the best cures in the doctor's book.   -Irish Proverb

I have found out that there ain't no sure way to find out whether you like people or hate them than to travel with them.   -Mark Twain

Friends are relatives you make for yourself.

          -Eustache Deschamps

One man can be a crucial ingredient on a team, but one man cannot make a team.   -Kareem Abdul-Jabbar

You are only what you are when no one is looking.

          -Unknown

Keep thy shop and thy shop will keep thee.

          -Proverb

For every problem God permits us to have, there is a solution.   -Thomas Edison

I expect to pass through this world but once. Any good therefore that I can do, or any kindness that I can show to my fellow-creature, let me do it now. Let me not defer or neglect it, for I shall not pass this way again.

-Stephen Grellet

A book lying idle on a shelf is wasted ammunition.

-Henry Miller

Every job is a self-portrait of the person who does it. Autograph your work with excellence.

-Unknown

If you go out looking for friends, you're going to find they're very scarce. If you go out to be a friend, you'll find them everywhere.   -Zig Ziglar

Whoever gossips to you will gossip about you.

-Spanish Proverb

Man creates culture and through culture creates himself.

-Pope John Paul II

Each child is an adventure into a better life – an opportunity to change the old pattern and make it new.

-Unknown

Wisdom is the wealth of a great leader.   -Proverb

If the camel gets his nose in the tent, his body will soon follow.   -Arab Proverb

He who does not trust enough will not be trusted.
     -Lao Tzu

We can do anything we want to do if we stick to it long enough.   -Unknown

Failure is not bad if it doesn't get into your heart. Success is not bad if you don't let it go to your head.

-Unknown

The secret of success in life for a man to be ready for his opportunity when it comes.   -Benjamin Disraeli

He who sleeps in continual noise is awakened by silence.

-William Dead Howells

Grandparents remember hundreds of stories whether they actually happened or not. -Unknown

You can lead a horse to water, but you can't make him drink. -English Proverb

Failure is not bad if it doesn't get into your heart. Success is not bad if you don't let it go to your head.

-Unknown

The 'amen" of nature is always a flower.

-Oliver Wendell Holmes

Music washes away from the soul the dust of everyday life. -Berthold Auerbach

Religion is what keeps the poor from murdering the rich.

-Napoleon

Children have more need of models than of critics.

-Unknown

You cannot fill your belly by painting pictures of bread.

-Chinese Proverb

Never forget that everything Hitler did in Germany was legal.   -Martin Luther King Jr.

Never talk of being tired. Talking of being tired makes you tired.   -Unknown

Woe unto you when all men speak well of you.

-Jesus

If you lie down with dogs, you'll get up with fleas.

-Proverb

Pay attention to your enemies, for they are the first to discover you mistakes.   -Antisthenes

People are lonely because they build walls instead of bridges.　　　-Joseph Forest Newton

The test of a first-rate work is that you finish it.

-Unknown

All the forces in the world are not so powerful as an idea whose time has come.
-Victor Hugo

It's not the years in your life that count. It's the life in your years.　　　-Abraham Lincoln

Not your friend but your enemy will tell you who you are.

-Greek Proverb

If you learn from a defeat, you haven't really lost.
-Old Saying

Bad men leave their mark wherever they go.

-Chinese Proverb

A great man is always willing to serve others.

-Unknown

Take care of your body. It's the only place you have to live.   -Jim Rohn

Love does not make the world go around. Love is what makes the ride worthwhile.   -Franklin P. Jones

I use not only all the brains I have, but all I can borrow.

-Woodrow Wilson

Flattery is like perfume. The idea is to smell it, not swallow it.   -William Ralph

Never send a chicken to bring home a fox.

-Irish Proverb

Clear your mind of can't.   -Unknown

Laziness travels so slowly, that poverty soon overtakes him.   -Unknown

A mule makes no progress when he's kicking. Neither does a man.   -E.H. Cummings

Books are where things are explained to you. Life is where things are not.   -Julian Barnes

Being stubborn is a virtue when you are right; it's only a character flaw when you are wrong.

        -Chuck Noll

No clock is more regular than the belly.

        -French Proverb

Life is a coin. You can spend it anyway you wish, but you can only spend it once.   -Unknown

Be yourself and think for yourself; and while your conclusions may not be infallible, they will be nearer right than the conclusions forced upon you.
        -Elbert Hubbard

One meets his destiny often in the road he takes to avoid it.   -French Proverb

What sunshine is to flowers, smiles are to humanity. They are but trifles to be sure but scattered along life's pathway the good they do is inconceivable.   -Joseph Addison

There is a mighty lot of difference between saying prayers and praying.   -John G. Lake

Everyone can master a grief, but he that has it.

          -Shakespeare

There is no greater love than the love that holds on where there seems nothing left to hold on to.   -Unknown

The swiftest horse cannot overtake the word once spoken.

          -Chinese Proverb

When a man puts a limit on what he will do, he puts a limit on what he can do.   -Charles M. Schwab

Lend a horse and you may have back his skin.

-English Proverb

To love what you do and feel that it matters – how could anything be more fun?　　-Unknown

Ability is a poor man's wealth.　　　-Matthew Wren

Nobody's sweetheart is ugly.　　　-Dutch Proverb

God did not save you by grace to live a disgrace.

-Sentence Sermon

To carry a grudge is like being stung to death by one bee.

-William H. Walton

Dreams don't work unless you do.　　　-Unknown

Pay no attention to what critics say. There has never been a statue set up in honor of a critic.　　-Jan Sibelius

What happens to a man is less significant than what happens within him.   -Louis L. Mann

You have a rudder-like control on your life and you get that control largely by the goals you set with deep desire.
          -Earl Nightingale

Remember that failure is an event, not a person.
          -Unknown

The best things in life are free.   -Proverb

Definiteness of purpose is the starting point of all achievement.   -Clement Stone

Efficiency is doing things right. Effectiveness is doing the right thing.   -Unknown

Behavior is a mirror in which everyone shows his true image.   -Johann Von Goethe

We, whoever we are, must have a daily goal in our lives, no matter how small or great, to make that day mean something. -Maxwell Maltz

Do not speak of your happiness to a man less fortunate than yourself. -Plutarch

Courage is like love, it must have hope for nourishment.

-Napoleon

Frequent kisses end in a baby. -Hungarian Proverb

Opportunities are seldom labeled. -John A. Shedd

The wise man reads, both books and life itself.

-Lin Yutang

I would rather think of life as a good book. The further you get into it, the more it begins to come together and make sense. -Rabbi Harold Kusher

Courage is not the absence of fear, but rather the judgment that something else is more important than fear.

-Unknown

Limitations are but boundaries created inside our minds.

-Unknown

Any garment will fit one who is naked.

-Chinese Proverb

When you're finished changing, you're finished.

-Benjamin Franklin

Laziness is nothing more than resting before you work.

-Jules Renard

About the only thing that comes to us without any effort is old age.   -Gloria Pitzer

People will rarely remember your advice, but they will always remember that you listened.

-Cara Lawrence

Character is made by what you stand for; reputation by what you fall for.   -Unknown

Repetition is the mother of learning.   -Russian Proverb

If there's hope in the future there is power in the present.
     -John Maxwell

Laughter adds richness, texture and color to otherwise ordinary days.   -Unknown

Choose a job you love and you will never have to work a day in your life.   -Confucius

Experience is not what happens to a man; it's what a man does with what happens to him.   -Aldous Huxley

Reward sweetens labor.   -Dutch Proverb

Money is a wonderful thing, but it is possible to pay too high a price for it.   -Alexander Bloch

Goals are dreams with deadlines. -Unknown

The one who snores the loudest will fall asleep first.
-Chinese Proverb

Distrust all men in whom the impulse to punish is powerful. -Friedrich Nietzsche

The wise does at once what the fool does at last.
-Unknown

Bind together your spare hours by the cord of some definite purpose. -W.M. Taylor

Tradition is the democracy of the dead.
-G.K. Chesterton

Be like a postage stamp — stick to one thing till you get there. -Unknown

If you cry because the sun has gone out of your life, your tears will prevent you from seeing the stars.

-Rabindranath Tagore

Our birth made us mortal, our death will make us immortal.   -Proverb

Laughter is sunshine in a house.   -Unknown

Nearly all men can stand adversity, but if you want to test a man's character, give him power.

-Abraham Lincoln

The present is the point at which time touches eternity.

-C.S. Lewis

When I rest, I rust.   -German Proverb

God can do nothing for me until I get to the limit of the possible.   -Oswald Chambers

The person who knows "how" will always have a job. The person who knows "why" will always be his boss.

-Unknown

Joy and sadness come by turn.   -Walker Perry

You see an awful lot of smart guys with dumb women, but you hardly ever see a smart woman with a dumb guy.

-Erica Jong

Develop the hunter's attitude. . . wherever you go, there are ideas waiting to be discovered.   -Unknown

Grandma and grandpa's house where the great are small, and the small are great.   -Unknown

There is a time to let things happen and a time to make things happen.   -Hugh Prather

Getting an idea should be like sitting down on a pin; it should make you jump up and do something.

-E. L. Simpson

Great men never know they are great.

-Chinese Proverb

A rumor is about as hard to unspread as butter.

-Proverb

Step by step, little by little, bit by bit – that is the way to wisdom that is the way to glory.   -Unknown

In the kingdom of the blind men, the one-eyed is king.

-Proverb

Do what we can, summer will have its flies.

-Ralph Waldo Emerson

Young man, the secret of my success is that at an early age I discovered I was not God.   -Oliver Wendell Holmes

The dictionary is the only place that success comes before work. Hard work is the price we must pay for success.   -Unknown

It isn't what the book costs; it's what it will cost if you don't read it.   -Jim Rohn

Right makes might.   -Proverb

Honor is better than honors.   -Unknown

Complainers are the greatest persecutors.

-Samuel Butler

Music is the medicine of a troubled mind.

-Walter Haddon

Beware of no man more than yourself; we carry our worst enemy with us.   -Charles Spurgeon

It is not what a man does that determines whether his work is sacred or secular, it is why he does it.

-Unknown

Every road has two directions.   -Russian Proverb

It's just like magic. When you live by yourself, all your annoying habits are gone.   -Merrill Markoe

No person was ever honored for what he received; honor has been the reward for what he gave.

-Calvin Coolidge

He who is outside his door has the hardest part of his journey behind him.   -Flemish Proverb

It is natural to make mistakes; it is terribly wrong to willfully keep making mistakes.   -St. Augustine

It is one of the most beautiful compensations of this life that no man can sincerely try to help another without helping himself.   -Ralph Waldo Emerson

A good sermon leaves you wondering how the preacher knew all about you.   -Anon.

Diligence is the mother of good fortune.

-Unknown

None is so deaf as those who won't hear. None so blind as those who will not see.   -Proverb

Unhappiness is in not knowing what we want and killing ourselves to get it.   -Unknown

The best form of flattery is to master the art of listening.
        -Chinese Proverb

He who foresees calamities suffers them twice over.
        -Portecus

Adversity has the effect of eliciting talents that in times of prosperity would have lain dormant.   -Horace

Early to bed early to rise, makes a man healthy, wealthy and wise.   -Benjamin Franklin

The difference between rising at five and seven o'clock in the morning for forty years, supposing a man to go to bed at the same hour at night, is nearly equivalent to the addition of ten years in a man's life.   -Doldridge

Every great institution is the lengthened shadow of a single man. His character determines the character of the organization.   -Ralph Waldo Emerson

Maturity doesn't come with age; it comes with acceptance of responsibility.   -Unknown

There is no hill without a valley.   -Proverb

Why stay we on earth except to grow?

-Robert Browning

A wise man cares not for what he cannot have.

-George Herbert

Family faces are magic mirrors looking at people who belong to us; we see the past, present and future.

-Gail Lumet Buckley

Happiness is as a butterfly, which when pursued, is always just beyond our grasp, but which if you will sit down quietly, may alight upon you.

-Nathaniel Hawthorne

Night conceals a world but reveals a universe.

-Robert Browning

The happiest people don't necessarily have the best of everything. They just make the best of everything.

-Unknown

We make a living by what we get, we make a life by what we give.   -Norman MacEwan

Make all you can, save all you can, and give all you can.

-John Wesley

Ask the experienced rather than the learned.

-Arabic Proverb

One of the difficult tasks in this world is to convince a woman that even a bargain costs money.

-Ed Howe

He who has a why to live can bear almost any how.

-Unknown

You cannot change your destination overnight, but you can change your direction overnight.   -Jim Rohn

As long as you can still be disappointed, you are still young.   -Sarah Churchill

There is no use in going back for a lost opportunity, someone else has already found it.

-Unknown

I don't know jokes; I just watch the government and report the facts.   -Will Rogers

Of all things you wear, your expression is the most important.   -Unknown

Remember, happiness doesn't depend upon who you are or what you have; it depends solely upon what you think.

-Dale Carnegie

A man's treatment of money is the most decisive test of his character – how he makes it and how he spends it.

-Unknown

One who thinks that money can do everything is likely to do anything for money.   -Anon.

It is better to be short of cash than to be short of character.   -Unknown

The plans of the diligent lead to profit as surely as haste leads to poverty.   -King Solomon

If the only prayer you say in your whole life is "Thank you," that would suffice.   -Meister Eckhart

I must govern the clock, not be governed by it.
          -Unknown

Adam ate the apple and our teeth still ache.
          -Hungarian Proverb

Adversity is a mirror that reveals one's true self.
          -Unknown

There's no fool like an old fool – you can't beat experience.   -Jacob M. Braude

Nothing is particularly hard if you divide it into small jobs.

    -Unknown

Great hate follows great love.   -Irish Proverb

Too bad all the people who know how to run the country are busy driving taxicabs and cutting hair.

    -George Burns

Better to remain silent and be thought a fool than to speak out and remove all doubt.   -Abraham Lincoln

It is the character of very few men to honor without envy a friend who has prospered.   -Unknown

Dream lofty dreams, and as you dream, so you shall become.   -James Allen

Clean hands are better than full hands.   -Proverb

If you would not be forgotten as soon as you are dead and rotten, either write things worth reading or do things worth writing.   -Benjamin Franklin

Positive thinking will let you do everything better than negative thinking will.   -Zig Ziglar

The same fence that shuts others out shuts you in.
     −Bill Copeland

There's one thing worse than being alone, wishing you were.   -Bob Steele

The most wasted of all days is that on which one has not laughed.   -Unknown

You can accomplish more in one hour with God than one lifetime without Him.   -Unknown

In anger, a person becomes a danger to himself and to others.   -Chinese Proverb

A man will fight harder for his interests than for his rights.

-Napoleon

Tomorrow is often the busiest time of the year.

-Spanish Proverb

Trials are blessings in disguise.   -Unknown

Beware every time you notice yourself doing a good thing because you ruin it by the notice.

-Oswald Chambers

Writing is a struggle against silence.

-Carlos Fuentes

All experience is an arch to build upon.

-Henry Brooks Adams

Lack of homework shows up in the workplace as well as in the classroom.   -Unknown

God does not comfort us to make us comfortable, but to make us comforters.   -J. H. Jowett

There is a close correlation between getting up in the morning and getting up in the world.   -Unknown

Everyone must row with the oars he has.

          -English Proverb

Ninety-nine percent of failures come from people who have the habit of making excuses.

          -George Washington Carver

Life is not measured by the number of breaths we take, but by the moments that take our breath away.

          -Maya Angelou

The first step on the way to victory is to recognize the enemy.   -Unknown

The grand essentials to happiness in this life are something to do, something to love, and something to hope for.   -Joseph Addison

All things are difficult before they are easy.   -Proverb

Success depends on backbone, not wishbone.

    -Unknown

The greatest dreams are always unrealistic.

    -Will Smith

Don't be afraid of opposition. Remember a kite rises against, not with the wind.   -Hamilton Mabie

There is in this world no such force as the force of a man determined to rise.   -Unknown

Learning preserves the errors of the past as well as its wisdom.   -Alfred North Whitehead

The road to hell is paved with good intentions.

    -Proverb

Happiness is not something you find, but rather something you create.   -Unknown

Politeness goes far, yet costs nothing.

 -Mademoiselle de Lambert

Not to have had pain is not to have been human.

 -Jewish Proverb

Learn by experience – preferably other people's.
 -Unknown

If a bird is flying for pleasure it flies with the wind, but if it meets danger it turns and faces the wind in order that it may rise higher.   -Corrie Ten Boom

Adversity causes some men to break; others to break records.   -Unknown

Fear defeats more people than any other one thing in the world.   -Ralph Waldo Emerson

You will get much more done if you crack the whip at yourself.   -Donald Laird

He that has learned to obey will know how to command.
     -Solon

Men are alike in their promises. It is only in their deeds that they differ.   -Unknown

Give him enough rope and he'll hang himself.
     -English Proverb

Whether you think you can or think you can't – you are right.   -Henry Ford

Conquer yourself rather than the world.
     -Unknown

Men love with their eyes. Women love with their ears.
     -Unknown

Winning is not everything, but making the effort to win is.

-Vince Lombardi

You must have long-range goals to keep you from being frustrated by short-range failures.   -Unknown

He who is slow in his work becomes poor, but the hand of the ready worker gets in wealth.   -King Solomon

At that point in life where your talent meets the needs of the world, that is where God wants you to be.

-Albert Schweitzer

A man is not honest simply because he never had a chance to steal.   -Russian Proverb

The most valuable of all talents is that of never using two words when one will do.   -Unknown

There was never a good war, or a bad peace.
-Benjamin Franklin

There's a time when you have to explain to your children why they're born, and it's a marvelous thing if you know the reason.   -Unknown

We generally change ourselves for one of two reasons: inspiration or desperation.   -Jim Rohn

If you control yourself in one moment of anger, you will escape a hundred days of sorrow.   -Chinese Proverb

When one is out of touch with oneself, one cannot touch others.   -Anne Morrow Linbergh

The mother's love is like God's love; He loves us not because we are loveable, but because it is His nature to love, and because we are His children.   -Unknown

Everyone should have a goal for which he is willing to exchange a piece of his life.   -Carlyle Boehme

Men go abroad to wonder at the heights of mountains, at the huge waves of the sea, at the long courses of the rivers, at the vast compass of the ocean, at the circular motions of the stars and they pass by themselves without wondering.　　　　-St. Augustine

A great man is always willing to be little.

　　　-Unknown

A day's work is a day's work, neither more nor less, and the man who does it needs a day's sustenance, a night's repose and the due leisure, whether he be painter or ploughman.　　　　-George Bernard Shaw

The heart has eyes that the brain knows nothing of.

　　　-Charles Henry Parkhurst

The true measure of a man is not in the number of servants he has, but in the number of people he serves.

　　　-Arnold Glasgow

An unused life is an early death.　　　　-Unknown

Shun idleness; it is rust that attaches itself to the most brilliant metals.   -Voltaire

In the long run men hit only what they aim at.

-Henry David Thoreau

When a man succeeds he does it in spite of everybody and not with the assistance of everybody.

-Edgar Watson Howe

The innkeeper loves the drunkard, but not for a son-in-law.   -Yiddish Proverb

He who would be a good leader must be prepared to deny himself much.   -Unknown

There was never a good war, or a bad peace.

-Benjamin Franklin

We sleep but the loom of life never stops; and the pattern that was weaving when the sun went down is weaving when it comes up tomorrow.   -Henry Ward Beecher

Some people succeed because they are destined to, but most people succeed because they are determined to.

-Unknown

Leadership is action, not position.   -Donald H. McGannon

What makes resisting temptation difficult for many people, is that they don't want to discourage it completely.

-Franklin P. Jones

Whatever your lot in life, build something on it.

-Unknown

Some men see things as they are and say, "Why?" I dream things that never were and say, "Why not?"

-George Bernard Shaw

Don't throw away the old bucket until you know whether the new one holds water.   -Swedish Proverb

Temptations without, imply desires within.

-Unknown

A man who does not read good books has no advantage over the man who can't read.   -Mark Twain

Divorce is spelled selfishness on the part of one party, sometimes both.   -Unknown

Always be a first-rate version of yourself, instead of a second-rate version of somebody else.

   -Judy Garland

Insults are the arguments employed by those who are in the wrong.   -Jean Jacques Rousseau

There never has been accomplished any great thing without first a man dreaming a dream or having a vision of it.   -Unknown

Necessity never made a good bargain.
   -Benjamin Franklin

Once you say you're going to settle for second, that's what happens to you in life, I find.

   -John F. Kennedy

Life can't give me joy and peace, it's up to me to will it.
Life just gives me time and space; it's up to me to fill it.

-Unknown

He has achieved success who has lived well, laughed
often, and loved much.   -Robert Louis Stevenson

A man who commits a mistake but doesn't correct it, is
making another mistake.   -Confucius

Water that does not move is always shallow.

-Proverb

Don't let life discourage you; everyone who got where he
is had to begin where he was.   -Richard l. Evans

Loneliness is the first thing God named, "not good."

-John Milton

Men for the sake of getting a living forget to live.

-Unknown

The minute you choose to do what you really want to do, it's a different kind of life.   -Buckminster Fuller

The mind is everything. What you think you become.
          -Buddha

Everything that irritates us about others can lead us to an understanding of ourselves.   -Unknown

It's not whether you get knocked down. It's whether you get up again.   -Vince Lombardi

Believe a boaster as you would a liar.   -Italian Proverb

The size of your success is determined by the size of your belief.   -Unknown

Experience is a hard school but a fool will learn in no other.   -Irish Proverb

The income tax has made liars out of more Americans than golf.   -Will Rogers

Be great in the little things.   -Anon.

A man wrapped up in himself makes a very small bundle.
        -Benjamin Franklin

I have held many things in my hands and lost them all;
but the things I have placed in God's hands those I always
possess.   -Unknown

The two most important days in your life are the day you
are born and the day you find out why.

        -Mark Twain

Many times the difference between your accomplishment
and your failure is your attitude.   -Zig Ziglar

Whose bread I eat, his song I sing.   -German Proverb

Anger is a luxury one cannot afford.

        -Chinese Proverb

We improve ourselves by victories over our self. There must be contests, and we must win.   -Unknown

If you burn your neighbor's house it doesn't make your home look better.   -Lou Holtz

I have had more trouble with myself than with any other man I have ever met.   -Dwight L. Moody

Triumph is just "umph" added to try.   -Unknown

Fields are won by those who believe in winning.

-Thomas Wentworth Higginson

Not until we are lost do we begin to understand ourselves.

-Henry David Thoreau

All happy families resemble one another, each unhappy family is unhappy in its own way.   -Leo Tolstoy

There is no failure except in no longer trying.

-Unknown

Abstinence is the best medicine. -Indian Proverb

Confidence cannot be produced by compulsion. Men cannot be forced to trust. -Daniel Webster

Without continual growth and progress, such words as improvement, achievement, and success have no meaning.

-Benjamin Franklin

Show me the man you honor, and I will know what kind of man you are. -Thomas Carlyle

You cannot steal second base while keeping one foot on first base. -Unknown

Education is that which remains when one has forgotten everything he learned in school.

-Albert Einstein

The deepest principle in human nature is the craving to be appreciated.   -William James

Laziness is a secret ingredient that goes into failure. But it's only kept a secret from the person who fails.

    -Robert Half

Nothing great was ever achieved without enthusiasm.

    -Ralph Waldo Emerson

True education is awakening a love for truth, the opening of the eyes of the soul to the great purpose and end of life.   -Unknown

For unto whosoever much is given, of him shall be much required: and to whom men have committed much, of him they will ask the more.   -Jesus

To eat one must chew, to speak one must think.

    -Proverb

There is nothing that makes men rich and strong but that which they catty inside of them. Wealth is of the heart, not of the hand.   -John Milton

Advice is what we ask for when we already know the answer but wish we didn't.   -Erica Jong

The burden is light on the shoulder of another.

   -Russian Proverb

Many an academic giant is also a spiritual midget, and if that be the case, he is usually a moral weakling as well.

   -Unknown

Do good with what thou hast; or it will do thee no good.

   -William Penn

Laziness is often mistaken for patience.   -Unknown

A good deed is never lost; he who sows courtesy reaps friendship and he who plants kindness gathers love.
   -Basil

A kind word never broke anyone's mouth.

-Irish Proverb

Men make houses but women make homes.
-Anon.

Marriage is a lot like the army, everyone complains, but you'd be surprised at the large number that re-enlist.

-James Garner

Many a man has found the acquisition of wealth only a change, not an end, of miseries.   -Unknown

You are either a product of your culture or your Creator.

-Cary Schmidt

If your foot slips, you may recover your balance, but if your tongue slips, you cannot recall your words.

-Martin Vanbee

Success seems to be largely a matter of hanging on after others have let go.   -Unknown

Patience is bitter, but its fruit is sweet.

-Jean Jacques Rousseau

Those who flee temptation generally leave a forwarding address. -Lane Olinghouse

If you keep saying that things are going to be bad, you have a chance of being a prophet. -Unknown

Persistent kindness conquers the ill-disposed.

-Ciero

In trying times don't quit trying. -Unknown

Never cut what you can untie. -Joseph Joubert

When a toothache comes, you forget your headache.

-Yiddish Proverb

A man is not old till regrets take the place of dreams.

-John Barrymore

If a task is once begun never leave it till it's done. Be the labor great or small, do it well or not at all.   -Proverb

A good deed is never lost; he who sows courtesy reaps friendship and he who plants kindness gathers love.
    -Unknown

All women become like their mothers. That is their tragedy. No man does. That's his.   -Oscar Wilde

It is not enough to be busy. The question is what are we busy about?   -Henry Ward Thoreau

No is one of the few words that can never be misunderstood.   -Unknown

Use self-control with your remote control.
    -Sentence Sermon

Optimism unaccompanied by personal effort is merely a state of mind and not fruitful.   -Edward L. Curtis

Form a habit of making decisions when your spirit is fresh...to let dark moods lead is like choosing cowards to command armies.   -Charles Horton Cooley

Kind words can be short and easy to speak but their echoes are truly endless.   -Unknown

Judge your natural character by what you do in your dreams.   -Ralph Waldo Emerson

You are never too old to set another goal or to dream a new dream.   -C.S. Lewis

Beware of little expenses; a small leak will sink a great ship.   -Benjamin Franklin

That which is beautiful is not always good. But that which is good is always beautiful.   -Chinese Proverb

A house is made of walls and beams; a home is made of love and dreams.   -Unknown

Those who know do not tell; those who tell do not know.

-Lao Tzu

If you give a mouse a cookie, he's going to want a glass of milk.   -Laura Joffe Numeroff

Don't mistake courtesy for consent.   -Unknown

The best way to hold your spouse is in your arms.

-Unknown

You may find the worst enemy or best friend in yourself.

-English Proverb

Know yourself. Don't accept your dog's admiration as conclusive evidence that you are wonderful.

-Ann Landers

The indispensable first step to getting the things you want out of life is this: Decide what you want.

-Ben Stein

Ninety percent of friction of daily life is caused by the wrong tone of voice.   -Unknown

Be yourself. No one can ever tell you you're doing it wrong.   -James Leo Herlthy

There is no rule without exception.   -English Proverb

The trouble with most people isn't so much their ignorance, as knowing so many things that ain't so.

        -Josh Billings

Everybody is ignorant, only on different subjects.

        -Will Rogers

Everyone has patience. Successful people learn to use it.

        -Unknown

To earn more you must learn more.   -Brian Tracy

Life can only be understood backwards, but it must be lived forwards.   –Soren Kierkegaard

I am always ready to learn, but I do not always like being taught.   -Winston Churchill

I am not responsible for my feelings, only for what I do with them.   -Ceophus Martin

Watch for temptation – the more you see of it the better it looks.   -Unknown

Be slow to promise but quick to perform.   -Chinese Proverb

A happy person is not a person in a certain set of circumstances, but rather a person with a certain set of attitudes.   -Hugh Downs

Give to the poor and you will never be in need. If you close your eyes to the poor, many people will curse you.

          -King Solomon

Each moment of the year has its own beauty, a picture which was never before and shall never be seen again.

-Ralph Waldo Emerson

A baby is born with a need to be loved and never outgrows it. -Frank A. Clark

We fear the government may be powerful enough to destroy our families, we know that it is not powerful enough to replace them. -Ronald Reagan

You cannot do a kindness too soon because you never know how soon it will be too late. -Unknown

Faith is seeing the invisible, but not the nonexistent.

A.W. Tozer

Where there is no shame there is no honor.

-German Proverb

Those who deny freedom to others, deserve it not for themselves. -Abraham Lincoln

My obligation is to do the right thing. The rest is in God's hands.   -Unknown

We rule the world with our words.

-Napoleon Bonaparte

Luck is a matter of preparation meeting opportunity.

-Elmer G. Letterman

Carve your name on hearts and not on marble.

-Charles Spurgeon

The bridge you burn now may be the one you later have to cross.   -Unknown

Not everyone who dances is glad.   -French Proverb

I wanted to change the world. But I have found that the only thing one can be sure of changing is ones' self.

-Aldous Huxley

Preconceived notions are the locks on the door to wisdom.   -Mary Browne

Forget yourself for others and others will not forget you.

-Unknown

Comfort comes as a guest, lingers to become a host and stays to enslave us.   -Lee Bickmore

One's own thoughts is one's own world. What a person thinks is what he becomes.   -Maitri Upanishads

I shall allow no man to belittle my soul by making me hate him.   -Booker T. Washington

Time ripens all things, no man is born wise.

-Miguel de Cervantes

Let your friends, colleagues and family know about the good that you see; it will help them see it too.

-Unknown

A baby is God's opinion that life should go on.

-Carl Sandburg

There are two ways of being happy. We must either diminish our wants or augment our means – either may do, the result is the same and it is for each man to decide for himself and to do that which happens to be easier.

-Benjamin Franklin

Decisions can take you out of God's will but never out of His reach.   -Unknown

Peace within makes beauty without.   -English Proverb

The healthy, the strong individual is the one who asks for help when he needs it. Whether he has an abscess on his knee or in his soul.   -Rona Barrett

Forgiveness is the key to action and freedom.

-Hannah Arendt

We all love that for which we sacrifice.   -Unknown

It is easier for a father to have children than for children to have a real father.   -Pope John XXIII

The springs of human action are inherently in the feelings, not the intellect.   -Unknown

The best way to make your dreams come true is to wake up.   -Paul Valery

If there is anything we wish to change in the child, we should first examine it and see whether it is not something that could better be changed in ourselves.

   -Carl Jung

The person who makes a success of living is the one who sees his goal steadily and aims for it unswervingly.

   -Cecil DeMille

A baby is something a mother carries inside of her for nine months, in her arms for three years, and in her heart till the day he dies.   -Unknown

A thorough knowledge of the Bible is worth more than a college education.   -Theodore Roosevelt

If a man could have half his wishes, he would double his troubles.   -Benjamin Franklin

It is easier to do a job right than to explain why you didn't.   -Martin Van Buren

Govern a family as you would cook a small fish – very gently.   -Unknown

Smooth seas do not make good sailors.   -Proverb

In business, there's such a thing as an invaluable person, but no such thing as an indispensable one.

     -Malcolm Forbes

Things have to be made to happen.   -Oral Roberts

Where there is room in the heart, there is room in the house.   -Thomas Moore

Conversation may enrich the understanding, but solitude is the school of genius.   -Gibson

Faith is daring the soul to go beyond what the eyes can see.   -Unknown

No fate is worse than a life without a love.   -Proverb

The chains of habit are generally too small to be felt until they are too strong to be broken.   -Samuel Johnson

Jealousy is the fun you think they had.

-Erica Jong

None are so empty as those who are full of themselves.

-Benjamin Whichcote

Good words are worth much, and cost little.

-Unknown

The intelligent man who is proud of his intelligence is like the condemned man who is proud of his large cell.

-Simone Well

Just don't give up trying to do what you really want to do. Where there is love and inspiration, I don't think you can go wrong. -Ella Fitzgerald

Many of life's failures are people who did not realize how close they were to success when they gave up.

-Thomas Edison

Often we change jobs, friends and spouses instead of ourselves. -Unknown

To attract attractive people, you must be attractive, to attract powerful people, you must be powerful. To attract committed people, you must be committed. Instead of going to work on them, you go to work on yourself. If you become, you can attract. -Jim Rohn

Whatever you can do, or dream you can do, begin it. Boldness has genius, power, and magic in it.

-Goethe

Better to be too skeptical than to be too trusting.

-Chinese Proverb

All of us will live forever – somewhere.   -Anon.

To carry care to bed is to sleep with a pack on your back.

-Thomas Haliburton

The things we remember best are those best forgotten.

-Blatasar Gracian

We are all born ignorant, but one must work hard to remain stupid.   -Benjamin Franklin

The only real peace in this world is peace of mind.

-Unknown

Your living is determined not so much by what life brings to you as by the attitude you bring to life; not so much by what happens to you as by the way your mind looks at what happens.   -John Homer Miller

No one is sadder than he who laughs too much.

-German Proverb

Any fact facing us is not as important as our attitude toward it, for that determines our success or failure.

-Norman Vincent Peale

Often, very often, we are punished as much by our sins as for them. -Unknown

Our opinion of people depends less upon what we see in them than upon what they make us see in ourselves.

-Sarah Grand

When you kill time you murder success.

-Sentence Sermon

Everybody thinks of changing humanity and nobody thinks of changing himself. -Leo Tolstoy

One-half the trouble of this life can be traced to saying yes too quick, and not saying no soon enough.

-Unknown

Misfortunes one can endure, they come from outside, they are accidents. But to suffer for one's own faults ah, there is the sting of life.   -Oscar Wilde

The man who has no imagination has no wings.

-Muhammed Ali

Get out of bed forcing a smile. You may not smile because you are cheerful; but if you will force yourself to smile you'll be cheerful because you smile. Repeated experiments prove that when man assumes the facial expression of a given mental mood, any given mood, then that mental mood itself will follow.   -Kenneth Goode

It's the job that's never started that takes longest to finish.

-Unknown

There are no illegitimate children, only illegitimate parents.

-Judge Leon Yankwich

Becoming active is the key remedy for depression.

-Pat Robertson

Work frees us from three evils: boredom, vice, and need.

-Voltaire

Business is like a wheelbarrow. Nothing ever happens until you start pushing.   -Unknown

God gives the nuts but He does not crack them.

-German Proverb

An eye for an eye makes the whole world blind.

-Gandhi

A family is a place where principles are hammered and honed on the anvil of everyday living.   -Unknown

A man ought to read as inclination leads him, for what he reads as a task will do him little good.

-Samuel Johnson

To be poor and independent is very nearly an impossibility.   -William Cobbert

The whole reason for juvenile delinquency is mental unemployment.   -Jackie Gleason

Fear of death is worse than death itself.   -Proverb

To bring up a child in the way he should go, travel that way yourself once in awhile.   -Unknown

Ain't no man can avoid being born average, but there ain't no man got to be common.   -Satchel Paige

A birthday is a good time to begin anew, throwing away the old habits, as you would old clothes, and never putting them on again.   -Bronson Alcott

Fears are educated into us and can, if we wish, be educated out.   -Unknown

Growth is the only evidence of life.

-John Henry Newman

The hardest thing to learn in life is which bridge to cross and which to burn.   -David Russell

That we should live forever is no greater miracle than that we should live at all.   -Unknown

In the field of observation, chance favors the prepared mind.   -Louis Pasteur

Things turn out best for the people who make the best of the way things turn out.   -John Wooden

The future belongs to those who believe in the beauty of their dreams.   -Eleanor Roosevelt

We do not remember days we remember moments.

-Unknown

The devil keeps school for neglected children.   -Anon.

Nothing is more important than what you expect. If you expect too little, you rob yourself.   -Robert Schuller

Do not pray for easy lives. Pray to be stronger men.

-John F. Kennedy

One wants to live and cannot, another can and will not.

-Yiddish Proverb

There is nothing either good or bad, but thinking makes it so.   -William Shakespeare

Often, very often, we are punished as much by our sins as for them.   -Unknown

A strong, positive self-image is the best possible preparation for success in life.   -Dr. Joyce Brothers

Presumption will bring nothing but trouble.

-Chinese Proverb

Let your children go if you want to keep them.

-Unknown

In life lots of people know what to do, but few people actually do what they know. Knowing is not enough. You must take action.   -Anthony Robbins

Love and romance is something everybody needs and that's regardless.   -Gertrude Berg

The world is full of willing people, some willing to work, the rest willing to let them.   -Unknown

You will find the key to success under the alarm clock.
-Benjamin Franklin

The only person who loves a change is a wet baby.

-Ray Blitzer

Discontent is the first step in the progress of a man or nation.   -Oscar Wilde

The most difficult secret for a man to keep is the opinion
he has of himself.   -Unknown

There is nothing so deceptive as an obvious fact.

    -Sir Arthur Conan Doyle

You don't have to burn books to destroy a culture. Just
get people to stop reading them.   -Ray Bradbury

The essence of generosity is self-sacrifice.

    -Henry Taylor

There is no poverty that can overtake diligence.

    -Unknown

A bad workman always blames his tools.

    -Proverb

Eternity is not something that begins after you are dead.
It is going on all the time. We are in it now.

    -Charlotte Gillman

Learn to say no, it will be of more use to you than to be able to read Latin.   -Charles Spurgeon

Never despair; but if you do, work on in despair.

-Unknown

It is wise to remember that you are one of those who can be fooled some of the time.   -Laurence J. Peter

The discontented man finds no easy chair.

-Benjamin Franklin

It is better to be a lender than a spender.
-Unknown

An apology is the superglue of life. It can repair just about anything.   -Lynn Johnston

The church is close, but the road is icy. The tavern is far, but I will walk carefully.   -Russian Proverb

Life has taught me that it is not for our faults that we are disliked and even hated, but for our qualities.

-Bernard Berenson

Many times our weaknesses are extensions of our strengths.   -Unknown

No one is useless in this world who lightens the burden of it to anyone else.   -Charles Dickens

Those who stand for nothing will fall for anything.

-Alexander Hamilton

One is given strength to bear what happens to one, but not the one hundred and one different things that might happen.   -C.S. Lewis

An hour of pain is as long as a day of pleasure.

-Proverb

Flatterers look like friends, as wolves like dogs.

-George Chapman

Too many talented people string and unstring their instruments without ever playing their music.

-Unknown

It is not the beard that makes the philosopher.

-Italian Proverb

We have to learn to be our own best friends because we fall too easily into the trap of being our worst enemies.

-Robert Thorpe

Good friends, good books, and a sleepy conscience. This is the ideal life.   -Mark Twain

A habit is a shirt made of iron.   -Harold Helfer

There is no such thing as standing still.   -Unknown

Live a life as a monument to your soul   -Ayn Rand

Any activity becomes creative when the doer cares about doing it right or better.   -John Updike

The pleasant future belongs to those who properly use today.   -Unknown

There is only one boss: the customer. And he can fire everybody in the company, from the chairman on down, simply by spending his money somewhere else.
                    -Sam Walton

Argue for your limitations and sure enough, they're yours.

          -Richard Bach

No one ever said on their deathbed: I wish I would have spent more time at work.   -Anon.

It's never wise to seek or wish for another's misfortune. If malice or envy were tangible and had a shape; it would be the shape of a boomerang.   -Charley Reese

Challenges are what make life interesting; overcoming them is what makes life meaningful.   -Joshua Marine

No illusion is more crucial than the illusion that great success and huge money buy you immunity from the common ills of mankind, such as cars that won't start.

-Larry McMurty

Adversity not only draws people together, but brings forth that beautiful inward friendship.   -Unknown

The most difficult thing in the world is to know how to do a thing and to watch someone else do it wrong without comment.   -T.H. White

The journey is what brings us happiness not the destination.   -Dan Millman

Appearances give us more pleasure than reality, especially when they help us satisfy our egos.
          -Unknown

Be wiser than other people, if you can, but do not tell them so.   -Lord Chesterfield

The man of fixed ingrained principles who has mapped out a straight course, and has the courage and self-control to adhere to it, does not find life complex. Complexities are all of our own making.   -B.C. Forbes

Throughout history 'tender loving care' has uniformly been recognized as a valuable element in healing.
        -Dr. Larry Dossey   .

Do not follow where the path may lead – go instead where there is no path and leave a trail.   -Unknown

A loan is like rice eaten. It is soon forgotten.
        -Chinese Proverb

There is one thing alone that stands the brunt of life throughout its length: a quiet conscience.

        -Unknown

When I have been unhappy, I have heard an opera…and it seemed the shrieking of winds, when I am happy, a sparrow's chirp is delicious to me. But it is not the chirp that makes me happy but I that make it sweet.

        -John Ruskin

A good neighbor doubles the value of a house.

-German Proverb

The difference between ordinary and extraordinary is that little extra.   -Unknown

Self-reliance is the only road to true freedom and being one's own person is its ultimate reward.

-Patricia Sampson

One man with courage makes a majority.   -Unknown

Give and it shall be given unto you.   -Jesus

The spirit of man is more important than mere physical strength, and spiritual fibre of a nation than its wealth.

-Dwight D. Eisenhower

Love is said to be blind, but I know lots of fellows in love who can see twice as much in their sweethearts as I can.

-Josh Billings

There is no hell like a bad conscience.   -John Crowne

When your image improves, your performance improves.
    -Unknown

Imagination is the true magic carpet.
    -Norman Vincent Peale

When a proud man hears another praised, he feels himself injured.   -English Proverb

Spite is never lonely, envy always tags along.
    -Unknown

Habit is habit, and not to be flung out of the window by any man, but coaxed downstairs a step at a time.
    -Mark Twain

The greatest things ever done on earth have been done little by little.   -Thomas Guthrie

If you don't stand for something you'll fall for anything.

-Unknown

Contentment makes poor men rich; discontent makes rich men poor.   -Benjamin Franklin

Many ideas grow better when transplanted into another mind than in the one where they sprang up.

-Oliver Wendell Holmes

The present is the outcome of the past; and it is the great hook upon which the future hangs.   -Unknown

Courage is what it takes to stand up and speak, courage is also what it takes to sit down and listen

-Winston Churchill

Too many people are thinking of security instead of opportunity. They seem more afraid of life than death.

-James Byrnes

In reading the lives of great men, I found that the first great victory they won was over themselves…self-discipline with all of them came first.　　-Harry S. Truman

What the teacher is, counts for more than what he says.
　　-Unknown

Evil enters like a needle and spreads like an oak tree.
　　-Ethiopian Proverb

Take calculated risks. That is quite different from being rash.　　-George Smith Patton Jr.

If you're in a card game and you don't know who the sucker is, you're it.　　-Unknown

Measure twice, cut once.　　-Craftsman Aphorism

Some things you have to do every day. Eating seven apples on Saturday night instead of one a day just isn't going to get the job done.　　-Jim Rohn

To keep a lamp burning we have to keep putting oil in it.

   –Mother Teresa

Live your questions now, and perhaps even without knowing it, you will live along some distant day into your answers.   -Rainer Maria Rilke

Have a heart that never burdens, a temper that never tires, a touch that never hurts.   -Charles Dickens

The ancestor of every action is a thought.

   -Ralph Waldo Emerson

Never think that you're not good enough yourself. A man should never think that. People will take you very much at your own reckoning.   –Anthony Trollope

Those that have done nothing in life are not qualified to be judge of those that have done little.   -Unknown

Love is like war, easy to begin but very hard to stop.

   -H.L. Mencken

The best way to predict the future is to create it.

-Peter Drucker

What history teaches us is that we have never learned anything from it. -George Wilhelm Hegel

He that is born to be hanged shall never drown.

-Proverb

A man never discloses his own character so clearly as when he describes another's. -Unknown

There are no embarrassing questions, only embarrassing answers. -Anon.

Train your child in the way in which you know you should have gone yourself. -Unknown

How far you go in life depends on you being tender with the young, compassionate with the aged, sympathetic with the striving, and tolerant of the weak and strong. Because someday in your life you will have been all of those.

-George Washington Carver

A country shall be judged by the quality of its proverbs.

-German Proverb

Character cannot be developed in ease and quite. Only through experience of trial and suffering can the soul be strengthened, ambition inspired, and success achieved.

-Helen Keller

The greatest use of life is to spend it for something that will outlast it.　　　-Unknown

Our bodies are our gardens – our wills are our gardeners.

–William Shakespeare

Ninety percent of the world's woe comes from people not knowing themselves, their abilities, their frailties, and even their real values.　　　-Sydney Harris

A man can't ride your back unless it's bent.
-Martin Luther King Jr.

Life is the greatest bargain, we get it for nothing.

-Yiddish Proverb

In the depth of winter I finally learned that there was in me an invincible summer.   -Albert Camus

We appreciate frankness from those who like us. Frankness from others is called insolence.   -Unknown

Where words fail, music speaks.   -Hana Christian Anderson

Envy is the art of counting the other fellow's blessings instead of your own.   -Harold Coffin

Do not believe those persons who say they have never been jealous. What they mean is that they have never been in love.   -Gerald Brenan

Lack of something to feel important about is almost the greatest tragedy a man may have.   -Unknown

For want of a nail the shoe was lost, for want of a shoe the horse was lost,: and for want of a horse the rider was lost; being overtaken and slain by the enemy, all for the want of care about a horseshoe nail.　　　　-Benjamin Franklin

Information is the currency of democracy.
　　　-Thomas Jefferson

The better we feel about ourselves the fewer times we have to knock somebody else down to feel tall.
　　　-Unknown

Impossible is not a fact. It's opinion. Impossible is not a declaration. It's a dare. Impossible is potential. Impossible is temporary. Impossible is nothing.
　　　-Muhammad Ali

It is just as easy to form a good habit as it is a bad one.
　　　-William McKinley

First you take a drink, then the drink takes a drink, then the drink takes you.　　　-F. Scott Fitzgerald

When going to an eating house, go to the one that is filled with customers.　　-Chinese Proverb

The more laws the more the offenders.

-Latin Proverb

Security is mostly a superstition. It does not exist in nature, nor do the children of men as a whole experience it. Avoiding danger is no safer in the long run than outright exposure. Life is either a daring adventure or nothing.　　-Helen Keller

You will make a lousy anybody else, but you are the best you in existence.　　-Unknown

The best way to succeed is to double your failure rate.

-Thomas Watson

Example is the school of mankind and they will learn at no other.　　-Edmund Burke

The years that a woman subtracts from her age are not lost. They are added to other women's.

-Diane De Poitiers

Without rest, a man cannot work, without work, the rest does not give you any benefit.   -Proverb

Never let a fool kiss you or a kiss fool you.

-Joey Adams

What we do on some great occasion will probably depend on what we already are; and what we are will be the result of previous years of self-discipline.   -Unknown

Be it ever so humble, there's no place like home.

-John Howard Payne

Man has his will, but woman has her way.

-Oliver Wendell Holmes

It is cheaper to give a small sum than to lend a large amount.   -Chinese Proverb

Example has more followers than reason and is more forcible than precept.   -Unknown

Men occasionally stumble over the truth, but most of them pick themselves up and hurry on as if nothing had happened.   -Winston Churchill

A smart wife sees through her husband. A good wife sees him through.   -Unknown

A woman is the only thing I am afraid of that I know will not hurt me.   -Abraham Lincoln

Education is the best provision for the journey to old age.

      -Aristotle

Income seldom exceeds personal development.
      -Jim Rohn

Never be haughty to the humble, never be humble to the haughty.   -Jefferson Davis

A man's reach should exceed his grasp.

-Unknown

It is extraordinary how extraordinary the ordinary person is.   -George F. Will

There are two things to aim at in life: first, to get what you want, and, after that, to enjoy it. Only the wisest of mankind achieve the second.
-Logan Pearsalli Smith

Every man's work whether it be literature, or music, or pictures, or architecture, or anything else, is always a portrait of himself.   -Unknown

It is necessary for us to learn from others' mistakes. You will not live long enough to make them all yourself.
-Hyman George Rickover

A wise man sees as much as he ought, not as much as he can.   -Michel de Montaigne

We probably wouldn't worry about what people think of us if we could know how seldom they do.   -Anon.

If you indulge in self-pity the only sympathy you can expect is from the same source.
     -Bill Copeland

Love looks through a telescope envy through a microscope.   -Unknown

We can often endure an extra pound of pain far more easily than we can suffer the withdrawal of an ounce of accustomed pleasure.   -Sydney Harris

Envy is like a disease it consumes the soul.
     -Jewish Proverb

Never feel self-pity, the most destructive emotion there is. How awful to be caught up in the terrible squirrel cage of self.   -Unknown

Habits are first cobwebs, then cables.
     -Spanish Proverb

A mind always employed is always happy. This is the true secret, the grand recipe, for felicity.
-Thomas Jefferson

You are a product of your own brainstorm.

-Rosemary Konner Steinbaum

He who seeks for applause only from without has all his happiness in another's keeping.
-Oliver Goldsmith

Drink does not drown care, but waters it, and makes it grow faster.   -Benjamin Franklin

Shallow men believe in luck...strong men believe in cause and effect.   -Emerson

All the trouble in the world is due to selfishness. It always has been and always will be.   -Joseph F. Flannely

There is always danger in extremes.   -Unknown

Our deeds determine us, as much as we determine our deeds.   -George Eliot

More flies are caught with a drop of honey than with a cask of vinegar.   -Dutch Proverb

The first duty of love is to listen.   -Unknown

What you do speaks so loud that I cannot hear what you say.   -Emerson

Defeat never comes to a man until he admits it.
          -Joseph Daniels

Children act in the village as they have learned at home.
          -Swedish Proverb

There is no other way by which any man can improve, except by experience.   -Unknown

To be upset over what you don't have is to waste what you do have.   -Ken Keyes Jr.

Only the wearer knows where the shoe pinches.

-Proverb

First say to yourself what you would be; and then do what you have to do.   -Unknown

Love is the irresistible desire to be irresistibly desired.

-Robert Frost

The biggest failure of all is the person that never tries.
-Dr. Larry Kimsey

Do not be tricked by false words: evil company does damage to good behavior.   -Bible

Never argue at the dinner table, for the one who is not hungry gets the best of the argument.

-Richard Whately

He who does not grow, declines.   -Anon.

Experience enables you to recognize a mistake when you make it.   -Franklin P. Jones

It only takes one lie to taint your entire testimony.

-Unknown

The best wine is the oldest, the best water is the newest.
-William Blake

If you want to be the best, you have to do things that other people aren't willing to do.
-Michael Phelps

The childhood shows the man, as morning shows the day.
-John Milton

The man who views the world at 50 the same as he did at 20 has wasted thirty years of his life.

-Muhammad Ali

The man who insists upon seeing with perfect clearness before he decides, never decides. Accept life, and you must accept regret. —Henri Frederic Amiel

A wolf may lose its fangs, but not its inclinations.

-Chinese Proverb

The things which hurt instruct. -Benjamin Franklin

Man cannot degrade woman without himself falling into degradation; he cannot elevate her without at the same time elevating himself. -Alexander Walker

Life is a dream for the wise, a game for the fool, a comedy for the rich, a tragedy for the poor. -Sholom Aleichem

All virtue is summed up in dealing justly. -Unknown

He who does not grow, declines. -Rabbi Hillel

Better lose the saddle than the horse. -Italian Proverb

And in the end it's not the years in your life that count. It's the life in your years.   -Abraham Lincoln

No matter what a man's past may have been, his future is spotless.   -Unknown

Dost thou love life? Then do not squander time, for that is the stuff life is made of.   -Benjamin Franklin

The eye is the window of the soul, even an animal looks for a man's intention right into his eyes.

     -Hiram Powers

Don't let your learning lead to knowledge, let your learning lead to action.   -Unknown

Men are nicer to the women they don't marry.   -Anon.

Maturity is achieved when a person accepts life as full of tension.   -Joshua Loth Liebman

What is written on sand is washed out by the sea.

-Proverb

On matters of style, swim with the current, on matters of principle, stand like a rock. -Thomas Jefferson

Good for the body is the work of the body, good for the soul the work of the soul, and good for either the work of the other. -Henry David Thoreau

War is the remedy that our enemies have chosen, and I say let us give them all they want. -William Sherman

Every failure is a step to success. -William Whewell

He has great tranquility of heart who cares neither for the praises nor the fault-finding of men. -Honore de Balzac

Some things have to be believed to be seen.

-Unknown

Well done is better than well said. -Benjamin Franklin

One reason why birds and horses are not unhappy is because they are not trying to impress other birds and horses.   -Dale Carnegie

You are never a loser until you quit trying.
      -Mike Ditka

A sincere compliment is one of the most effective motivational methods in existence.
      -Unknown

You don't get to choose how you're going to die. Or when. But you can decide how you're going to live now.
      -Joan Baez

It is better to lose than to win an unjust or dishonest cause.   -Unknown

The life of the creative man is led, directed and controlled by boredom. Avoiding boredom is one of our most important purposes.   -Saul Steinberg

Please all and you will please none.   -Proverb

The price of success, freedom, and economic independence is high, but not nearly so high as the price of failure, bankruptcy, heavy indebtedness, and worry.

-Unknown

It is not the strongest of the species that survive, nor the most intelligent, but the one most responsive to change.

-Leon Magginson

Self-pity in its early stages is as snug as a feather mattress. Only when it hardens does it become uncomfortable. -Maya Angelou

A fair exterior is a silent recommendation.

-Publilius Syrus

Self-respect is the fruit of discipline; the sense of dignity grows with the ability to say no to oneself.

-Abraham Joshua Heschel

Habit if not resisted soon becomes necessity.

-St Augustine

It is far more impressive when others discover your good qualities without your help.   -Judith Martin

One who would pick the roses must bear with the thorns.

-Chinese Proverb

Adam was the luckiest man: he had no mother-in-law.
-Sholom Aleichem

Marriage is wonderful. Without it husbands and wives would have to fight with strangers.
-Morey Amsterdam

The miracle of the seed and the soil is not available by affirmation; it is only available by labor.

-Jim Rohn

Attitude determines altitude. Outlook determines outcome.

-Unknown

A candle lights others and consumes itself.

-Proverb

The best armor is to keep out of range.

-Italian Proverb

Bitterness is the offspring of an unhealed wound, whose parents are unforgiveness and time.   -Unknown

What is difficult? To keep a secret, to employ leisure well, to be able to bear an injury.   -Chilon

Those who move the easiest are those who have learned to dance.   -Alexander Pope

Character is doing what's right when nobody's looking.

-Unknown

Better the devil you know than the devil you don't know.

-Proverb

The only way to prove you are a good sport is to lose.

-Ernie Banks

He who gambles picks his own pocket.   -Anon.

One of life's great rules is this: The more you give, the more you get.   -Unknown

What I kept I lost. What I spent I had. What I gave I have.
          -Proverb

When you teach your son, you teach your son's son.
          -The Talmud

Honesty is the first chapter in the book of wisdom.
          -Thomas Jefferson

Procrastination is the thief of time.   -Unknown

It's no disgrace to be poor, but it's no great honor, either.
          -Sholom Aleichem

Honesty is the first chapter in the book of wisdom.

-Thomas Jefferson

We are involved in a life that passes understanding; our highest business is our daily life.   -John Cage

Forget your opponents; always play against par.

-Unknown

We often give our enemies the means of our own destruction.   -Proverb

Human felicity is produced not so much by great pieces of good fortune that seldom happen, as by little advantages that occur every day.   -Benjamin Franklin

Public opinion is like the castle ghost, no one has ever seen it, but everyone is scared of it.   -Sigmund Graff

The most effective persuasion is a life well lived.

-Unknown

Labor disgraces no man, unfortunately, you occasionally find men disgrace labor.   -Ulysses S. Grant

One cannot always be a hero, but one can always be a man.   -Johann Wolfgang Von Goethe

Dollars cannot buy yesterday.   -Old Saying

Prosperous times are when the foundation of failures are laid.   -Proverb

It's hard to beat a person who never gives up.   -Babe Ruth

There may be people that have more talent than you, but there's no excuse for anyone to work harder than you do.   -Derek Jeter

Compromise is always a temporary achievement.   -Chinese Proverb

If a man achieves success and does not blend into his life a program of self-improvement to bring about a sensible balance, he no doubt will end up as a failure.

-Unknown

Snowflakes are one of nature's most fragile things but just look at what they can do when they stick together.
-Vesta Kelly

Your time is limited, so don't waste it living someone else's life.　　　　　-Steve Jobs

Example is not the main thing influencing others. It is the only thing.　　　　　-Albert Schweitzer

The laughter of a child is music to a parent's ear.

-Unknown

There is only 3 colors, 10 digits, and 7 notes; it's what we do with them that's important.　　　　　-Jim Rohn

We are born helpless. As soon as we are fully conscious we discover loneliness. We need others physically, emotionally, intellectually, we need them if we are to know anything, even ourselves.   -C.S. Lewis

A well trained memory is one that permits you to forget everything that isn't worth remembering.

          -Unknown

What is defeat? Nothing but education, nothing but the first step to something.   -Wendell Philips

An army of sheep led by a lion would defeat an army of lions led by a sheep.   -Arab Proverb

Pain is temporary. It may last a minute, or an hour, or a day, or a year, but eventually it will subside and something else will take its place. If I quit, however, it lasts forever.

          -Lance Armstrong

Forgive and you shall be forgiven.   -Jesus

Never play not to lose; always play to win.   -Old Saying

The distance a man has got on his journey is of less consequence than the direction in which his face is turned.   -Alexander Maclaren

I'm not afraid to die. I just don't want to be there when it happens.   -Woody Allen

Movement is a medicine for creating change in a person's physical, emotional, and mental states.
          -Carol Welch

Defeat is not the worst of failures. Not to have tried is the true failure.   -Unknown

There are lots of people who mistake their imagination for their memory.   -Josh Billings

When someone sings his own praises, he always gets the tune too high.   -Mary H. Waldrip

Character is a by-product; it is produced in the great manufacture of daily duty.   -Woodrow Wilson

You do not lead by hitting people over the head – that's assault, not leadership.　　　-Unknown

I will prepare and someday my chance will come.

　　　-Abraham Lincoln

A dead thing can go with the stream, but only a living thing can go against it.　　　-G.K. Chesterton

An inconvenience is only an adventure wrongly considered.　　　-Unknown

Without leaps of imagination, or dreaming, we lose the excitement of possibilities. Dreaming, after all, is a form of planning.　　　-Gloria Steinem

It is not the size of a man but the size of his heart that matters.　　　-Evander Holyfield

Courage doesn't mean you don't get afraid. Courage means you don't let fear stop you.

　　　-Bethany Hamilton

One who learns the value of compromise acquires wisdom.   -Chinese Proverb

You grow up the first time you laugh at yourself.

-Unknown

The brain may be important, but the stomach is still in charge.   -Charles m. Schulz

One man with courage is a majority.

-Thomas Jefferson

Once you have accepted yourself, it's so much easier to accept other people and their points of view.

-Unknown

Pray, and let God worry.   -Martin Luther

Friends are the siblings God never gave us.

-Mencius

Home wasn't built in a day.   -Jane Ace

A learned blockhead is a greater blockhead than an ignorant one.   −Benjamin Franklin

Unless you try to do something beyond what you have already mastered you will never grow.   -Unknown

Imagination is more important than knowledge.
          -Albert Einstein

The nice thing about egotists is that they don't talk about other people.   -Lucille S. Harper

The hypocrite's crime is that he bears false witness against himself.   -Hannah Arendt

Everything that is done in the world is done by hope.
          -Martin Luther

I would rather fail in the cause that someday will triumph than triumph in a cause that someday will fail.

-Unknown

Vows are made in storms and forgotten in calms.

-Proverb

If you will set the example, you won't need to set many rules.   -Zig Ziglar

Getting married is easy. Staying married is more difficult. Staying happily married for a lifetime should rank among the fine arts.   -Roberts Flack

The easiest way to destroy a man's faith is to destroy his morality.   -Unknown

The real man is one who always finds excuses for others but never excuses himself.   -Henry Ward Beecher

Always acknowledge a fault frankly. This will throw those in authority off their guard and give you opportunity to commit more.   -Mark Twain

When you are younger you get blamed for crimes you never committed and when you're older you begin to get credit for virtues you never possessed, it evens itself out.
-George Santayana

One who learns the value of compromise acquires wisdom.   -Chinese Proverb

As iron sharpens iron, so a friend sharpens a friend.
-Solomon

Unless you try to do something beyond what you have already mastered you will never grow.   -Unknown

The man who trims himself to suit everybody will soon whittle himself away.   -Charles Schwab

One man with courage is a majority.

-Andrew Jackson

A wager is a fool's argument.   -Proverb

Destiny is not a matter of chance, it is a matter of choice. It is not a thing to be waited for; it is a thing to be achieved. -William Jennings Bryan

Life is an echo. What you send out – you get back. What you – give you get. -Anon.

I've missed more than 9,000 shots in my career. I've lost almost 300 games. 26 times, I've been trusted to take the game winning shot and missed. I've failed over and over and over again in my life. And that is why I succeed.

-Michael Jordan

Everything comes to those who can wait.

-French Proverb

We don't stop playing because we grow old; we grow old because we stop playing. -George Bernard Shaw

When it is obvious that the goals cannot be reached, don't adjust the goals, adjust the action steps.

-Confucius

Time is all you have. And you may find one day that you have less than you think.　　　　　-Randy Pausch

Water is the only drink for a wise man.
　　　-Henry David Thoreau

Every one desires to live long, but no one would be old.
　　　-Abraham Lincoln

A good marriage would be between a blind wife and a deaf husband.　　　-Michael de Montaigne

I cannot live without books.　　　-Thomas Jefferson

Routine is a condition of survival.　　　-Flannery O'Conner

Hedges have eyes and walls have ears.　　　-Proverb

Nothing but religious faith has been able to save men from despair.　　　-Unknown

A long journey tests a horse; a long-drawn-out conflict tests a friendship.   -Chinese Proverb

You can easily judge the character of a man by how he treats those who can do nothing for him.   -Unknown

Life's tragedy is that we get old too soon and wise too late.   -Benjamin Franklin

Life is like playing a violin in public and learning the instrument as one goes on.   -Samuel Butler

Love is an act of endless forgiveness, a tender look that becomes a habit.   -Unknown

The best security for old age, respect your children.

          -Sholem Asch

Nothing happens unless first a dream.

          -Carl Sandburg

At the touch of love, everyone becomes a poet.

-Plato

Vanity is the result of a delusion that someone is paying
attention.   -Paul E. Sweeney

What life does to us in the long run depends upon what
life finds in us.   -E. Stanley Jones

Imagination was given to man to compensate him for what
he is not. A sense of humor was provided to console him
for what he is.   -Unknown

Being cheerful keeps you healthy. It is slow death to be
gloomy all the time.   -King Solomon

What was hard to bear is sweet to remember.

-Portuguese Proverb

A man can never be a true gentleman in manner until he
is a true gentleman at heart.   -Charles Dickens

Conceit is a weird disease. It makes everybody sick, except the one who's got it.   -Zig Ziglar

All men are caught in an inescapable network of mutuality.   -Martin Luther King Jr.

Everything that was ever accomplished on the face of this earth was achieved with the same equipment that you possess.   -Herbert Kaufman

When spiders unite, they can tie down a lion.

-Ethiopian Proverb

It is hard to be a child, just remember you were a child once.   -Unknown

One of the greatest obstacles to a man's advancement is discontent.   -Henry Ford

Act the part and you will become the act.

You miss 100 percent of the shots you don't take.

-Wayne Gretzky

Stupidity is too often beauty's imperfection.
-French Proverb

The entire water of the sea can't sink a ship unless it gets inside the ship. Similarly, negativity of the world can't put you down unless you allow it to get inside you.

-Unknown

One reason why I don't drink is because I wish to know when I'm having a good time.   -Nancy Astor

The quality of your life is determined by the quality of your time management.   -Brian Tracy

Settle a small conflict quickly and you will keep a hundred at bay.   -Chinese Proverb

Success seems to be largely a matter of hanging on after others have let go.   -Unknown

There is a homely old adage which runs: "Speak softly and carry a big stick; you will go far."

-Theodore Roosevelt

It is better to offer no excuse than a bad one.

-George Washington

Little minds are tamed and subdued by misfortune; but great minds rise above them.   -Unknown

Winning doesn't start around you – it begins inside you.

-Mike Murdock

Time is the main ingredient for accomplishing great things.   -Unknown

A danger foreseen is half avoided.

-Thomas Fuller

It is not by the gray of the hair that one knows the age of the heart.   -Edward Bulwer-Lytton

Kites rise highest against the wind, not with it.

-Unknown

The better part of one's life consists of his friendships.
-Abraham Lincoln

You are not only responsible for what you say, but also for what you do not say.　　　-Martin Luther

Men today are losing faith in themselves because they have lost faith in God.　　　-Unknown

Life consists not only in holding good cards but in playing those you hold well.　　　-Josh Billings

The best way to lose weight is to eat all you want of everything you don't like.　　　-Max Asnas

Leadership is the challenge to be something more than average.　　　-Jim Rohn

A modest man is usually admired – if people ever hear of him.   -Ed Howe

Imagination offers people consolation for what they cannot be, and humor for what they actually are.

-Albert Camus

The dead take to the grave, clutched in their hands, only what they have given away.   -DeWitt Wallace

The sovereign invigorator of the body is exercise, and of all the exercises walking is the best.

-Thomas Jefferson

Would you live with ease, do what you should, and not what you please. Success has ruined many a man.

-Benjamin Franklin

A man should live with his superiors as he does with his fire, not too near, lest he burns; nor too far off, lest he freeze.   -Albert Pike

I like liquor – its taste and its effects – and that is just the reason why I never drink it. -Stonewall Jackson

The ideal man bears the accidents of life with dignity and grace, making the best of the circumstances.

-Aristotle

In the life of a true believer there are no accidents.

-Corrie ten Boom

We remain great by doing the same things we did to become great. -Dr. Judson Mitchell

Far and away the best prize that life offers is the chance to work hard at work worth doing.

How much better is it to get wisdom than gold and to get understanding rather to be chosen than silver!

-King Solomon

Autobiography in Five Short Chapters

I walk down the street

There is a deep hole in the sidewalk.

I fall in. I am lost...I am hopeless.

It isn't my fault.

It takes forever to get out.

I walk down the same street.

There is a deep hole in the sidewalk.

I pretend I don't see it. I fall in again.

I can't believe I am in the same place.

But it isn't my fault.

It still takes a long time to get out.

I walk down the same street.

There is a deep hole in the sidewalk.

I see it there. I still fall in...it's a habit.

My eyes are open. I know where I am.

It's my fault. I get out immediately.

I walk down the same street.

There is a deep hole in the sidewalk.

I walk around it.

Now I walk down another street.

-Dr. Charles L. Whitefield

Concluding Words

11 The sayings of wise men are like the sharp sticks that shepherds use to guide sheep, and collected proverbs are as lasting as firmly driven nails. They have been given by God, the one Shepherd of us all.

12 Son, there is something else to watch out for. There is no end to the writing of books, and too much study will wear you out.

13 After all this, there is only one thing to say: Have reverence for God, and obey his commands, because this is all that man was created for.

14 God is going to judge everything we do, whether good or bad, even things done in secret.

-King Solomon   (Eccl 12:11-14 TEV)

About The Author

Ruben Martinez is an ordained minister. He has been studying the Bible for over thirty years. He currently pastors a church in Phoenix Arizona. He lives in the Phoenix area with his wife; they have been happily married for thirty-seven years.

www.ingramcontent.com/pod-product-compliance
Lightning Source LLC
Chambersburg PA
CBHW072123280526
45788CB00002B/517